# Breaking Bad

## I AM THE DANGER

RUNNING PRESS
PHILADELPHIA • LONDON

Books published by Running Press are available at special discounts
for bulk purchases in the United States by corporations, institutions, and other
organizations. For more information, please contact the Special Markets
Department at the Perseus Books Group, 2300 Chestnut Street,
Suite 200, Philadelphia, PA 19103, or call (800) 810-4145, ext. 5000, or e-mail
special.markets@perseusbooks.com.

ISBN 978-0-7624-5110-4
Library of Congress Control Number: 2013951961

E-book ISBN 978-0-7624-5319-1

9   8   7   6   5   4   3   2   1
Digit on the right indicates the number of this printing

Cover and Interior Design by Jason Kayser
Edited by Jennifer Leczkowski
Typography: Pill Gothic

Running Press Book Publishers
2300 Chestnut Street
Philadelphia, PA 19103-4371

Visit us on the web!
www.runningpress.com

**"TECHNICALLY, CHEMISTRY IS THE STUDY OF MATTER. BUT I PREFER TO SEE IT AS THE STUDY OF CHANGE. IT IS GROWTH, THEN DECAY, THEN TRANSFORMATION."**

o says Walter White, high school chemistry teacher at J.P. Wynne High School in Albuquerque, New Mexico. His life drastically changes when he is diagnosed with stage III lung cancer and given a prognosis of two years to live. Using his expert chemistry knowledge, he begins producing and selling methamphetamine with his former student, Jesse Pinkman, in order to secure his family's financial future. With a new sense of fearlessness, Walt embarks on a journey of power, corruption, and lies and evolves from a normal family man to a criminal mastermind, all the while maintaining that everything he has done has been for his family.

Now you can relive some of the most powerful events from this journey through not only Walter White's words, but also through the words of the people whose lives were inexorably transformed by him. Full of iconic character quotes and images from all seasons, this companion book recalls many of the exciting and unforgettable moments that are *Breaking Bad*.

WALT:
DID YOU LEARN
NOTHING
FROM MY CHEMISTRY
CLASS?

JESSE:
NO, YOU FLUNKED ME,
REMEMBER?

SOME STRAIGHT LIKE YOU, GIANT STICK UP HIS ASS AND ALL THE SUDDEN AT AGE, WHAT, 60, HE'S JUST GONNA BREAK BAD?

—JESSE

YOU WANNA
COOK?

—WALT

SHUT THE
FUCK UP
AND LET ME DIE
IN PEACE.

—MIKE

THIS MONEY,
I DIDN'T STEAL IT.
IT DOESN'T
BELONG TO
ANYONE ELSE.
I EARNED IT.

—WALT

# WELL, IT'S JUST
## BASIC CHEMISTRY, YO.

—JESSE

WE GOT NEW PLAYERS
IN TOWN. WE DON'T KNOW
WHO THEY ARE, WHERE
THEY COME FROM…
BUT THEY POSSESS AN
EXTREMELY HIGH SKILL SET.
ME PERSONALLY? I'M
THINKING ALBUQUERQUE
JUST MIGHT HAVE A
NEW KINGPIN.

—HANK

SOMETIMES
YOU GOTTA ROB
TO KEEP
YOUR RICHES.

—TUCO

YOU MAY KNOW
A LOT ABOUT
CHEMISTRY, MAN,
BUT YOU DON'T
KNOW JACK ABOUT
SLINGING DOPE.

—JESSE

SO YOU DO
HAVE A PLAN.

YEAH, MR. WHITE!

YEAH, SCIENCE!

—JESSE

JESSE:
# HOW MUCH CASH DO YOU NEED?

WALT:
# MORE.

TO ALL LAW
ENFORCEMENT
ENTITIES, THIS IS
NOT AN ADMISSION
OF GUILT. I AM
SPEAKING TO MY
FAMILY NOW.

—WALT

WHAT DOES
A MAN DO,
WALTER? A MAN
PROVIDES FOR
HIS FAMILY.

—GUS

THERE IS NO
YOUR HALF OF THE
MONEY. THERE
IS ONLY MY
ALL OF IT. DO YOU
UNDERSTAND?

—WALT

I'M SLINGING MAD
VOLUME AND FAT
STACKING BENJIES, YOU
KNOW WHAT I'M
SAYING? I CAN'T
BE ALL ABOUT, LIKE
SPELLING, AND SHIT.

—SKINNY PETE

THE
CHEMISTRY
MUST
BE
RESPECTED.

—WALT

I'M A
BLOWFISH.
YEAH!
BLOW FISHING
THIS UP!

—JESSE

YOU ARE NOT
THE GUY. YOU'RE NOT
CAPABLE OF BEING
THE GUY. I HAD
A GUY BUT NOW
I DON'T. YOU ARE
NOT THE GUY.

—MIKE

JESSE:
NOW, WE'RE GONNA
BE KINGS, UNDERSTAND.
WELL, I'M GONNA
BE KING, YOU GUYS
WILL BE PRINCES OR DUKES
OR SOMETHING.

BADGER:
I WANNA BE A KNIGHT.

SERIOUSLY, WHEN THE GOING GETS TOUGH, YOU DON'T WANT A CRIMINAL LAWYER. YOU WANT A "CRIMINAL" LAWYER.

—JESSE

SO IF YOU WANNA
MAKE MORE MONEY
AND, UH, KEEP THE
MONEY YOU MAKE...

## BETTER CALL SAUL!

—SAUL

LOOK, WE ARE IN THIS FIFTY-FIFTY. OKAY?

—WALT

# STAY OUT

## —— OF ——

# MY TERRITORY.

—WALT

LET'S JUST SAY I KNOW A GUY WHO KNOWS A GUY. WHO KNOWS ANOTHER GUY.

—SAUL

JESSE:
**IT'S ALL ABOUT
ACCEPTING WHO YOU
REALLY ARE.
I ACCEPT WHO I AM.**

WALT:
**AND WHO ARE YOU?**

JESSE:
**I'M THE BAD GUY.**

THIS IS MILLIONS, UNCLE JACK. NO MATTER HOW MUCH YOU GOT, HOW DO YOU TURN YOUR BACK ON MORE?

—TODD

THIS FAMILY IS EVERYTHING TO ME. WITHOUT IT, I HAVE NOTHING TO LOSE.

—WALT

WALT:
HONESTY IS GOOD.
DON'T YOU
THINK?

SKYLER:
I FUCKED TED.

YOU KNOW,
WALTER, SOMETIMES
IT DOESN'T HURT
TO HAVE SOMEONE
WATCHING
YOUR BACK.

—MIKE

FACING DEATH,
IT CHANGES
A PERSON.
IT HAS TO, DON'T
YOU THINK?

—MARIE

I'M GONNA SHOW
YOU JUST HOW
WRONG YOU
ARE AND THEN I'M
PUTTIN' THAT BULLET
IN YOUR HEAD
MYSELF.

—JACK

DON'T DRINK
AND DRIVE,
   BUT IF YOU DO,

## CALL ME.

—SAUL

I LOVE THE LAB.
BECAUSE IT'S
ALL STILL MAGIC.
YOU KNOW?

—GALE

THIS IS MY
OWN PRIVATE
DOMICILE
AND I WILL NOT
BE HARASSED.
BITCH.

—JESSE

BOTH OF YOU
THINK YOU'RE GOING
TO JUST WALK
AWAY FROM THIS
THING? NEVER.
GONNA. HAPPEN.

—HANK

YO, ADRIAN,
ROCKY CALLED,
HE WANTS
HIS FACE BACK.

—SAUL

I GUESS
CRIME DOES
PAY.

—SKYLER

YOU TWO
SUCK AT
PEDDLING METH.
PERIOD.

—SAUL

# I HIDE IN PLAIN SIGHT,

## SAME AS YOU.

—GUS

# HELLO CAROL.

—WALT

YOU ARE A
WEALTHY MAN NOW.
AND ONE MUST
LEARN TO BE RICH.
TO BE POOR, ANYONE
CAN MANAGE.

—GUS

I'VE STILL
GOT
THINGS LEFT
TO DO.

—WALT

YOU KILL ME,
YOU HAVE NOTHING.
YOU KILL
JESSE, YOU
DON'T HAVE ME.

—WALT

JESSE:
WE'RE ALL ON THE
SAME PAGE.

WALT:
AND WHAT PAGE IS THAT?

JESSE:
THE ONE THAT SAYS:
"IF I CAN'T KILL YOU,
YOU'LL SURE AS SHIT WISH
YOU WERE DEAD."

YOU WON, WALTER.
YOU GOT THE
JOB. DO YOURSELF
A FAVOR AND LEARN
TO TAKE "YES" FOR
AN ANSWER.

—MIKE

HANK:

"W.W." . . . I MEAN, WHO DO YOU FIGURE THAT IS? WOODROW WILSON? WILLY WONKA? WALTER WHITE?

WALT:

HEH. YOU GOT ME.

THIS GENIUS
OF YOURS…
MAYBE HE'S STILL
OUT THERE.

—WALT

BELIEVE ME,
THERE'S NO
HONOR AMONG
THIEVES.
EXCEPT FOR
US, OF COURSE.

—SAUL

YOU CLEARLY DON'T KNOW
WHO YOU'RE TALKING TO
SO LET ME CLUE YOU IN.
I AM NOT IN DANGER, SKYLER.
I AM THE DANGER. A GUY
OPENS HIS DOOR AND
GETS SHOT, AND YOU THINK
THAT OF ME? NO. I AM THE
ONE WHO KNOCKS.

—WALT

SKYLER, THIS
IS A SIMPLE DIVISION
OF LABOR. I BRING
IN THE MONEY,
YOU LAUNDER THE
MONEY.

—WALT

MIKE:
ALL RIGHT,
WHAT'S THE
ORDER OF THE DAY?

JESSE:
EYES OPEN,
MOUTH SHUT.

# AM I UNDER ARREST?

—SKYLER

TIGHT, TIGHT, TIGHT! OH, BLUE, YELLOW, PINK. WHATEVER, MAN. JUST KEEP BRINGING ME *THAT*.

—TUCO

YOU TWO WANT TO STICK YOUR WANGS IN A HORNET'S NEST, IT'S A FREE COUNTRY, BUT HOW COME I GET SLOPPY SECONDS, HUH?

—SAUL

# DING DING DING

—TIO

SKYLER:
**WHAT HAPPENED?**

WALT:
# I WON.

SAY THE WORDS.
SAY YOU
WANT THIS.
NOTHING HAPPENS
UNTIL I HEAR
YOU SAY IT.

—JESSE

YOU ARE A TIME BOMB, TICK, TICK, TICKING, AND I HAVE NO INTENTION OF BEING AROUND FOR THE BOOM.

—MIKE

SHUT UP! SHUT UP!
SHUT UP! SHUT UP!
SHUT UP! SHUT UP!
SHUT UP! SHUT UP!
SHUT UP! SHUT UP!
SHUT UP! SHUT UP!

—SKYLER

JUST BECAUSE
YOU SHOT JESSE
JAMES DOESN'T
MAKE YOU
JESSE JAMES.

—MIKE

WALT:
**WHAT ARE
YOU WAITING FOR?**

SKYLER:
**FOR THE CANCER TO
COME BACK.**

I AM IN THE
**EMPIRE**
BUSINESS.

—WALT

WALT:
SAY MY NAME.

DECLAN:
YOU'RE
HEISENBERG.

WALT:
YOU'RE GODDAMN
RIGHT.

YOU'RE MY FREE PASS, BITCH.

—JESSE

WALT . . . I WANT MY
KIDS BACK. I WANT
MY LIFE BACK.
PLEASE TELL ME.
HOW MUCH IS ENOUGH?
HOW BIG DOES THIS
PILE HAVE TO BE?

—SKYLER

IF YOU DON'T
KNOW WHO I AM,
THEN MAYBE
YOUR BEST COURSE
WOULD BE TO

TREAD
LIGHTLY.

—WALT

JUST TELL ME YOU
DON'T GIVE A SHIT ABOUT
ME, AND IT'S EITHER
THIS OR YOU'LL
KILL ME THE SAME
WAY YOU KILLED MIKE.

—JESSE

**YOU KILLED UNCLE HANK. YOU KILLED HIM.**

—WALT JR.

**IT CAN'T ALL BE FOR NOTHING! PLEASE. PLEASE.**

—WALT

TALENT LIKE THAT
AND HE FLUSHES
IT DOWN THE
CRAPPER. IT'S LIKE
MICHELANGELO
WON'T PAINT.

—SAUL

THIS IS JUST A HEADS UP
TO LET YOU KNOW I'M
COMING FOR YOU. SEE,
I DECIDED THAT BURNING
DOWN YOUR HOUSE IS
NOTHING. NEXT TIME I'M
GOING TO GET YOU WHERE
YOU REALLY LIVE.

—JESSE

YOU'RE THE SMARTEST
GUY I EVER MET,
AND YOU'RE
TOO STUPID TO SEE.
HE MADE UP HIS MIND
TEN MINUTES AGO.

—HANK

CHEER UP,
BEAUTIFUL PEOPLE.
THIS IS WHERE
YOU GET TO
MAKE IT RIGHT.

—WALT

**BADGER:**
YOU KNOW, I DON'T EXACTLY KNOW HOW TO FEEL ABOUT THIS.

**SKINNY PETE:**
FOR REAL, YO. THE WHOLE THING FELT KINDA SHADY. YOU KNOW, LIKE MORALITY-WISE.

# WE'RE DONE WHEN I SAY WE'RE DONE.

—WALT

I DID IT FOR ME.
I LIKED IT.
I WAS GOOD AT IT.
AND I WAS REALLY…
I WAS ALIVE.

—WALT